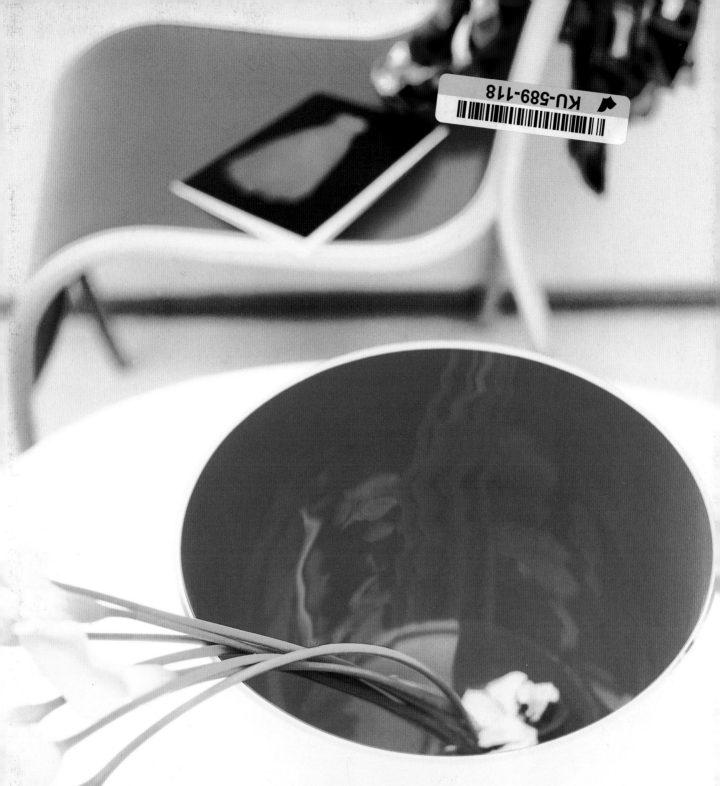

KU-589-118

PRIVATE VIEW TRICIA GUILD

SPECIAL PHOTOGRAPHY BY JAMES MERRELL   TEXT WITH ELSPETH THOMPSON

CONTENTS

BLACKBURN COLLEGE
LIBRARY
Acc. No. BB01682
Class No. HSC 747.092 GUI
Date 04/05/05

INTRODUCTION

People say you are what you eat, but in my view you are what you see – or how you see...
Wherever we go, we are taking in glimpses, impressions, of the world around us, and I believe
that these images go deep into our psyches, becoming part of our own energy and
imagination... This applies to any kind of image – a still from a film, the proportions of a
doorway, reflections in the water, a misty evening when the light gives an extraordinary
atmosphere – all sorts of things that we see every day, or on travels to out-of-the-way
places... They build into a private pattern book of images, waiting to connect in some way.
Much later on, one of these images will come into my head, suggesting a combination of
colours, a pattern, an idea for a design. This is how inspiration works for me.

In this book I've tried to gather together some of my lasting passions: the images and
impressions that give me inspiration – spontaneous pieces of pattern that form a creative
process and inspire a visual expression of my feelings. I hope to convey in the following
pages the essence of how that works.

TRICIA GUILD

TRANSFORMING COLOUR

Where does one learn about colour? From the landscape; from nature; from looking at flowers and growing flowers; from rows of vegetables growing in a garden or piled on a stall in a food market. You learn by watching the changing light and its effects on your surroundings. You can never stop learning about colour. We experience colour all the time; we find new ways of seeing colour and new ways of being enlivened by it. To me it has always been one of the most truly life-enhancing aspects of being alive. Consider the colours on this page. Don't they make it so much more stimulating than seeing the words on plain white?

Choosing colours is a form of self-expression. We make decisions based on colour all the time – maybe a conscious decision such as what colour to paint a room or cover a sofa, or  an almost unconscious choice such as what colour toothbrush or washing-up bowl to buy. Some people think that they don't have

a colour sense, but I believe everybody has one – we are just not all in tune with it. Once you start to become aware, you realize that everyone has colours that wake them up, that make them feel happy, sad or balanced.

Colours can transform themselves with the changing light. This is one of the most fascinating and inspiring aspects of my work as a designer. Colour is light, or different wavelengths or vibrations of light. Morning light has a freshness all its own – colours and reflections are definitely clearer and purer than at other times, while afternoon light tinges everything with yellow or grey. Shadows are extraordinary in the way that they take on different colours. Think of shadows in the snow – what colour is the snow? An artist might use pink, mauve, blue – unexpected colours which at first might seem exaggerated, but which really are the natural colours at that particular moment.

Light can also transform the colours of the ocean – the sea feels positive and invigorating in the summer sun, when it is deep greeny blue, but on a stormy day it can feel quite threatening. In a similar way, a sudden shaft of sunshine, or the glow of a particular type of light bulb, can change the perceived colour of paint on a wall, or the stripes on a fabric, and in doing so change the entire mood of a room.

I can look at flowers for hours, trying to capture the colours and spirit of them in a way that can be translated to a textile design. Or I can be a simple observer, allowing all my senses to be stimulated as I become absorbed in the natural world. Take this incredibly graphic image of a butterfly. The combination of black and white and orange is so strong and powerful – colour is nothing without black and white. The image is sensual, romantic and graphic, all at the same time. And yet it is an apparently random design of nature. Sometimes the natural world is the best teacher. There is no such thing as a colour clash in nature.

MATISSE: COLOUR AND JOY

Q Can you sum up Matisse's appeal?

Matisse has been a great source of inspiration for me, for so many reasons. His colour sense is extraordinary; he used pattern, graphics, black and white; he could paint figures as well as still lifes; and whatever he painted, you could always feel the spirit in it. Whether it's an image for his book 'Jazz' (published in 1947), or a design for stained glass windows in the Chapel of Our Lady of the Rosary at Vence, in France, or a painting from Morocco, or a portrait of Madame Matisse – all his work has an extraordinary sense of colour and form. This is what continues to nourish me. Maybe it is inevitable that I would love Matisse's interior paintings. They seem to sum up everything I aim for when I design a room: the exuberant colours, the patterns, the mix of stripes and florals, fruits and flowers.

Q There is a great sense of spontaneity about his work, isn't there?

True, but that seeming effortlessness belies the

hard work and thought involved in everything he did. He said, "I have always tried to hide my efforts and wished my works to have the light joyousness of springtime, which never lets anyone suspect the labours it has cost me." That is certainly something one tries to emulate when creating an interior – that sense of effortlessness, that it has all come together naturally, without too much striving.

Q Matisse's works have an effect on all the senses, don't they?

Yes, I find that they have a strong emotional pull. For instance, even if it's an interior that he is depicting, he can so suffuse the painting with joy that you just want to be there. Immediately, you can feel the room, smell the fruit, taste the light – it is vibrant with life. Yet at the same time, the paintings are very contemporary, very graphic. They are about layers and layers of pattern, flat on the surface, with a lot of black and white, which

was really quite unusual at that time. And his drawings are full of grace and fluidity, it's as if his pencil never left the page. In just three lines he can portray a woman, or a face or a body. As he said, "A colourist makes his presence known even in a single charcoal drawing" . Even in old age, when he was too ill to paint, he developed paper cut-outs, using the same vivid colours and daring compositions, which an assistant could assemble for him. His passion to create was so strong that he was working until the day he died in 1954.

Q Are there other artists from the same period whose work you admire?

I find the paintings of the Fauves movement in the early 20th century – in particular what they were doing with colour – completely electrifying. Their use of non-naturalistic colours was one of the first avant-garde developments in European art, and the excitement still leaps off the canvas.

Inspiration from the calypso colours of the islands of the Caribbean – bright fabrics, dazzling sea and landscape, tropical fruit and flowers, the hustle

and good humour of the market place. All find their way by an indefinable process of osmosis into my work as a designer of fabric and wallpaper.

REMEMBERED COLOUR

The iridescent bright colours of tropical fish swimming in clear blue water... Flashes of fleeting brilliance... Where does inspiration come from? Perhaps it is about holding and staying true to the qualities of these remembered images.

A long way from tropical fish – and yet those flashes of orange against bright blue are behind the dynamic energy of this modern interior. Stretching a banner of bright flowered fabric at the floor-to-ceiling windows allows the light to filter through and further illuminate the colours. Touches of orange elsewhere – in the cushions, the flowers, the vases and the shiny surface of a moulded plastic chair – seem to float against the airy backdrop.

PATTERN

We are surrounded at times by shape, form and pattern: the patterns made by objects, the patterns of flowers, the patterns we make in a room. The delicate balance between shape, form and body gives interest to being in a house. Textiles – plain, textured, woven, patterns of geometrics and abstract painterly flowers, delicate handwoven embroideries, lustrous silks, spots and stripes – add to that richness, giving life to a space.

A pattern book of India: jewel-bright colours and intricate surface patterns of Indian miniatures in the City Palace in Jaipur… rose and marigold petals

as spiritual offerings... handpainted decorations on trucks and rickshaws... the crumpled silk of saris reflected in the tranquil backwaters of Kerala.

A PRESENT-DAY OFFERING

Pink ranunculus, pale green hellebores, marigolds and primulas pick out the clear

pastel colours of a votive picture bought at an Indian street market stall.

SPIRIT
OF JAPAN

These Japanese geisha girls speak of an extreme discipline, a ritualized form of beauty that is far removed from the way we live here in the West. We are so ready to reveal everything, while the geishas' beauty is always veiled beneath the layers of their garments – they do not even reveal their smiles. These clothes cannot just be thrown on; they are all part of an elaborate ritual that lifts even everyday activities out of the ordinary. Something of this spirit remains with the modern-day Japanese – in their tea ceremonies, in their gardens, in the way that they eat. It is the perfect counterbalance to the speed and consumerism that is also now a part of their culture.

PARIS

Timeless elegance, glamour and romance.

What

a wonderful

juxtaposition of old and

new. To take a classic, decorative

17th-century building like the Louvre and place in

the middle of it something so uncompromisingly modern,

which in no way takes away from the existing architecture, is an

extraordinary achievement. This is modern architecture at its absolute best – strong

yet delicate, graceful and disciplined – the perfect contrast to the embellished façades all

around it. I.M. Pei's work always has a quiet profundity about it – it is never showy or overemphasized. To

me he is one of the greatest modern architects. He felt that the pyramid itself was less important than the

re-organization of the entire museum around one central point, which is where the pyramid and new entrance now stand. The form

was the result of considering the pitch of the roofs all around: "The pyramid echoes the pitch of the roof... and it's the least obstructive of

form and space," he said. "If you put a cube there, you hide most of the Louvre... A cone is probably the best, but a cone is not a good form".

I.M. PEI'S LOUVRE PYRAMID

ARCHITECTURAL FORM

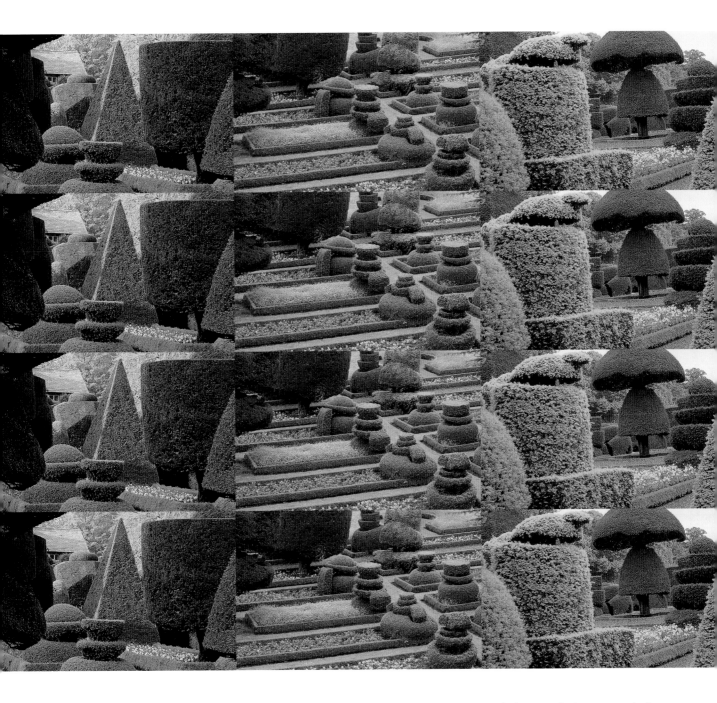

Topiary combines structure in a garden with eccentricity. The huddle of clipped shapes that surrounds Levens Hall in Cumbria is extraordinary: some are more than ten metres tall and have retained their strict geometric forms, while others have ballooned into amorphous shapes that resemble abstract sculpture. It was laid out as a fashionable 17th-century formal garden, with small clipped cones, obelisks and other shapes marking the corners of box-edged beds. But when formal gardens fell from favour and were ripped up to make way for the naturalistic landscape schemes of Capability Brown, those at Levens remained – and were left to grow and grow.

FRANK GEHRY

Frank Gehry's architecture is like abstract sculpture in the air. It never fails to startle and surprise, yet the curious curved forms carve their own comfortable space in the surrounding landscape, and the interiors never lose sight of the human scale and condition. In spite of their extreme radicalism, Gehry's buildings never seem to alienate the public. The Guggenheim Museum in Bilbao, Spain, must be one of the most remarkable buildings of our time.

BARBARA HEPWORTH

Look deep into the curves of a Barbara Hepworth sculpture and you can see the contours of a female body, the bones of the Cornish landscape. Hepworth was an early and courageous pioneer of abstract art in Britain and participated in various avant-garde groups such as Unit One, which in 1934 set out to embody "the expression of a truly contemporary spirit". Her statement in their catalogue sums up her concept of sculpture, to which she remained true until her death in 1975: "Carving is interrelated masses conveying an emotion; a perfect relationship between the mind and the colour, light and weight… so that it can exist in no other way, something completely the right size but which has growth, something still and yet having movement, so very quiet and yet with a real vitality." She was deeply affected by the dramatic scenery of Cornwall after she and her second husband, Ben Nicolson, moved to St Ives in 1939. "I am cradled in the anatomy of the landscape" she wrote. The Cornish cliffs and caves, hollowed by the rhythms of sea and wind, shadow and sunlight, became an intrinsic part of her work, to which she dedicated the remainder of her life. Something of her strong and unique spirit still inhabits the beautiful walled sculpture garden around her former studio in St Ives.

The old cars you see in the streets of Havana are so extraordinarily stylish. Ancient and

battered, creaking and cranking along, but carefully repainted and lovingly cared for, they are

a far cry from our fast-changing, throwaway culture, yet with more elegance than today's cars

could ever hope to attain. It's a new form of elegance, brought about partly by necessity, but

also through a continuing respect for the generous proportions, the beautiful forms and the

craftsmanship of the past. These old cars speak of an era that is fast disappearing, but is

kept alive by the right spirit, in certain corners of the world.

CUBAN CARS

LUIS BARRAGAN: MINIMALISM WITH SOUL

Q How would you describe your passion for Barragán's work?

What touches me most is that his work is so minimal and yet so full of soul. He used walls like sculpture, and colour to bring definition to the space. It is often thought that minimalist architecture has to be completely devoid of colour, but he embraced both – perhaps because of his upbringing in Mexico, where vibrant colour is such a strong part of life.

Q What is it about his colours that particularly inspires you?

The crucial thing is that his use of colour was never exaggerated or coarse. He has also taught me that while colour can be joyful and vibrant, like anything, if it is overused it negates itself. You need the contrast of white to allow the colour to be seen.

He used mostly hot colours, such as magenta, cobalt blue and ochre, but these would always be tempered by a softer shade and lots of white, and also by natural elements such as sand, stone, cobbles and water. For instance, at San Cristobal, just outside Mexico City, his

reinterpretation of a traditional farmhouse, water cascades from a wonderful persimmon-coloured chute into a pool of cool water enclosed by walls of cerise and white.

Q How did you feel when you visited his houses?

Sometimes when you go to places that you know from photographs it can be disappointing, but in this case it was completely the opposite. Because of his use of space, light and colour, his houses have a real energy and spirit about them. This had obviously also touched the current owners, as nothing had been altered – the furnishings, the gardens, the placing of a bowl of fruit – were all retained as a living homage.

Q Do you think his ideas can be translated to cultures and climates so different from his?

Absolutely. There is an assumption that you can't use colour in northern light, when in fact we need it more! People from warmer climates may find it easier to identify with colour, but it's definitely not exclusive – think of the way the Scandinavians and Irish have used colour in their homes. And even though his first house was built more than 60 years ago, there is a timelessness about Barragán's work that makes it still seem modern today.

Q How do you think his architecture has influenced you?

As Barragán himself said: "Beauty, inspiration, magic, sorcery, enchantment, and also serenity, mystery, silence, privacy, astonishment... All of these have found a loving home in my soul."

When I design I consider how a space feels and what it is like to live in, not just the surface details. Barragán's daring use of colour has made me more confident in my own approach to colour. I might look at a wall, whether it be in a Manhattan loft or

a French château, decide to paint just one wall in a particular colour, and it will change the emotional feel of the whole place.

FRIDA KAHLO: LIFE AS ART

Q Is it hard to separate Frida Kahlo as a woman from her art?

Her very way of living was an art form in itself. She was exuberant in the way she lived and dressed and in the home she created, and this vibrant life force seems to radiate from her work. There was, of course, a dark side to her life – the pain and turmoil of her chronic illness and her relationship with Diego Rivera – but this added another rich layer to all she achieved. Her love for Rivera was both fantastic and terrible: she was in physical or emotional pain for most of her life, and must have had the most extraordinarily strong will to have channelled it into her art. Her painting had an almost explosive quality: one critic described it as "like a ribbon around a bomb".

Q She was a one-off, then, impermeable to the vagaries of artistic fashion?

That is one of the factors that have made her appeal so lasting. Yes, she was a product of her time in one sense – in fact, she changed her date of birth to 1910 to affiliate herself with the Mexican Revolution of that year – but her originality and eccentricity would have made her stand out in any age. When I look at her and her work, I see this unique creative spirit that was stronger than time and fashion, stronger than anything that life could throw at her. You can see the human qualities in everything she created.

Q What did you think of her house?

Her home is Mexcico is every bit as unusual as you might hope or expect. The architecture is uncompromisingly modern, in glass and concrete, and is personalized by the use of colour – bright blue for Frida's house and pink for Rivera's next door. The two houses are linked by a bridge, and surrounded by a courtyard garden. The bright colour continues inside – lots of blue and yellow in Frida's kitchen, with traditional Mexican tiles, an eclectic mixture of old and new Mexican artefacts as well as the trappings of an international modern life. And, of course, her own work.

Q Has she not become most famous for her self-portraits?

Frida painted many self-portraits, most of

which had a very precise quality to the painting, not unlike that of miniatures. Picasso himself wrote to Rivera: "Neither you nor I can paint a head like Frida Kahlo". In many of her self-portraits the use of black is tremendously dramatic – you can really sense her eyes looking out from beneath those famous thick eyebrows. Sometimes she wears her own take on traditional Mexican costume, illustrating the unique alchemy by which she combined folklore and timeless tradition to produce a bold and thoroughly modern image.

MODERN CERAMICS

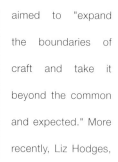

Gandhi

From Sevres to Delft, Carlton ware to Clarice Cliff, Roman glass to Venini – the sensuality and form of ceramics and glass have attracted artists of many disciplines. I collect work by artists such as Carol McNicoll, Janice Tchalenko, Liz Hodges and Linda Hoffhines, and we have struck up a friendship and working relationship that has continued for many years. We work together on one-offs or small productions that we can sell in the Designers Guild Store, making their work accessible to more people.

It seems commonplace today, but the Designers Guild Store was one of the first places where one could buy modern ceramics in a contemporary 'lifestyle' environment, rather than from a craft-orientated gallery.

The late 1970s was an interesting time for British ceramics: women artists in particular were breaking out of the studio tradition of simple organic shapes in brown earthenware exemplified by the work of Bernard Leach. Janice Tchalenko was one of the first ceramicists to use strong colour in earthenware – the secret of her brilliance was that she applied the glazes to a white ground, not straight on to the clay. Her shapes became more graphic to give the decoration full rein and, whereas most potters continued to decorate plates, bowls and jugs

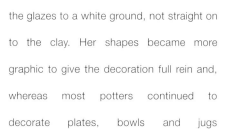

differently, according to tradition, Tchalenko developed an 'all-over' pattern more akin to fabric design. Her later work, whether stencilled or using lively freehand designs, has all the splashy brilliance of modern watercolours.

Carol McNicoll is another innovator whose work has embraced film, fashion and pop music as well as ceramics; she has always aimed to "expand the boundaries of craft and take it beyond the common and expected." More recently, Liz Hodges, Linda Hoffhines, Sophie Cook, Christiane Perrochin, Henriette Gaillard and others have continued the tradition of women potters breaking the mould. Many of them work in white, such as the cool one-off moulded pieces designed by

Rosaria Rattin for Kose and Sophie Cook's delicate vessels.

Glass is another great love, from the fluid forms, jewel-bright colours and innovative surface patterns of Venini designs in the 1950s to the luminosity of Ettore Sotsass's work for Memphis in the 1980s.

WHITE ON WHITE

MEMPHIS
GLASS

Ettore Sotsass, founder of the Memphis
Collective, was "an intellectual lightning rod"
for the young designers of his day, liberating
them from the dry traditionalism they had been
taught at college and enabling them to adopt
a more fluid, conceptual approach to design.
His own work embraced everything from the first
Italian calculator to Malpensa airport in Milan.

BRUCE McLEAN

Bruce McLean is one of Britain's most intriguing contemporary artists. Best known as an exciting and dynamic painter, he has worked in many other media, including glass and ceramics, as well as in innovative interior design schemes. His ceramics are very much an artist's response to the medium – more sculptural than crafted, with a quirky originality and subtle humour that is evident in the pieces shown here.

BUTTERF

How important black and white is to us! It's everywhere we look, from the painterly patterns on a butterfly's wings to everyday objects such as newspapers and zebra crossings. It's a classic combination that has been used in art and architecture by everyone from Masaccio to Mondrian to Le Corbusier and beyond.

MAKING A GARDEN

For me, a garden is outside space; living space that just happens to be outside. You plan it in the same way. The best gardens have structure – without that fundamental structure, whether it comes from trees, walls or hedges, they may never seem to come together.

You can always tell the difference between a garden made by a plantsman and one made by someone with more of an architectural vision. It's a bit like devoting yourself to the details of a room without thinking through the layout of the space; getting so carried away with the furniture, the paintings and the accessories that you forget how the space itself actually works. Or like choosing fabrics for your house – it is always better to work to an overall scheme. It may be seductive to buy one or two of every plant because they are all so beautiful, but this approach will not usually make a good garden, as it may not have the necessary strength. You have to be selective,

and that can sometimes be difficult.

That, to me, is why Vita Sackville-West's garden at Sissinghurst, in Kent, still holds such a remarkable appeal. It has both architectural structure and superb planting. Vita had a boldness of taste and sense of colour that perfectly complemented the strong lines of her husband's structural design. And she was completely ruthless about what plants went where and whether they stayed there – experimenting all the time and only keeping what worked.

These are some of the lessons that I have tried to follow when designing my own gardens. In all of them I have first thought about the structure. Our London garden (left and overleaf), which I created with the help of the designer Arne

Maynard, has very strong bones, with an inner square enclosure of pleached lime trees and lots of clipped box, yew and beech in balls, cubes and columns. I've also

learned that each plant has its own requirements. You can't force a plant to thrive in the wrong soil or aspect or in the wrong container – and you cannot expect it to do something that doesn't suit it.

In summer there are lots of flowers – roses and lavender and alliums and agapanthus and some wonderful clematis in all shades of purple, mauve and blue – but because of the structure, the garden looks good all year round, even in the dead of winter. In fact, I rather like it in winter,

with just the different shades of green.

In another part of the London garden is a tiny formal parterre with clipped box hedges, but all the compartments are filled with edible plants – herbs and artichokes and tomatoes in summer. Harvesting flowers, vegetables and fruit is a great joy. It's particularly pleasing when living in the city to be able to go outside in the evening and pick some herbs and vegetables to use immediately in cooking.

SUMMER IN THE CITY

Freshly picked vegetables, simply roasted with sprigs of home-grown herbs – all the abundant colours and textures of the kitchen garden, but here presented in a sophisticated urban setting.

ARNE MAYNARD: SPIRIT OF PLACE

To my mind, Arne Maynard is one of the most talented garden designers working in Britain today. Whether in the city or in the depths of the country, his gardens are a magical combination of architecture and romance, the classic and the contemporary, and relate to their surroundings in subtle ways. He has said: "A sense of place is the soul of the garden... the intangible and harmonious atmosphere that stems from a perfect balance between the house, garden, landscape, plants and, importantly, the dreams of the owner...." To create a sense of place one needs "a treasure chest of influences for your imagination to play with": his include childhood memories, art, architecture and wild nature. Arne's own garden (following pages), which he carved with his partner from the flat Fenlands of Lincolnshire, has a unique atmosphere that enchants all who visit it. I was lucky enough to see it in its earliest stages and have enjoyed following its progress from a few trees in a field to a series of formal yet romantic outdoor rooms surrounding the charming 17th-century brick house. Though the structure of the garden is quite classic, with ancient brick walls and smartly clipped hedges of box, beech and yew, there is always a contemporary twist to the planting, with fashionable deep reds and purples among the herbaceous borders, and key plants used in bold blocks and swathes rather than dotted here and there. The overall impression is of a place that somehow manages to combine romance and mystery with the clean, crisp lines of contemporary minimalism. He even manages to achieve this in his vegetable garden, which is one of the most beautiful that I have ever seen, with eccentric topiary spirals and fragrant dark sweet peas planted among the neatly ordered beds. We worked together to create a small London garden – and he immediately understood the atmosphere I was searching for.

FOOD FROM AN ENGLISH GARDEN

In early summer, what could be more delicious than cold pea soup with asparagus spears? Pouring the soup into glasses rather than bowls allows the spring green colour to be seen, with mint leaves adding a freshness that is perfectly in tune with the citrine yellows and pale greens of the glasses. Classic food becomes excitingly contemporary when arranged as a graphic picture on the table.

GREEN
LEAVES
LIFE
ENERGY
SIMPLICITY
GROWTH
BEAUTY

OUTDOOR LIVING

At our farmhouse in Tuscany, life spills outside into the garden all summer long. From early in the morning, when I like to work in the kitchen garden before the heat rises, to long leisurely alfresco lunches on the terrace, to drinks  beneath the trees when the sun is setting, the garden is the backdrop to our lives. Though some of the garden is quite wild, the areas nearer the house have been designed with some of the formal structure of 'rooms' with different uses and atmospheres. Between the house and the wilder lawns and orchard is a square gravel terrace that acts as an outdoor sitting room. The 'green architecture' of low box hedging contains the space, with topiary cones and spheres like living furniture or sculpture. Within this formal structure, tables and chairs are gathered in casual groups, and a mood of relaxed spontaneity prevails: it's the perfect place for reading the paper over coffee in the morning, or chatting to visitors in the

sunshine. I like to mix light contemporary pieces in plastic and metal with rustic antiques or one-off commissions. Bright striped fabrics are perfect for deckchairs or awnings to create more shade. For larger lunches or dinners, we lay a long table in the shade of trees and hang candle lanterns in the branches at night.

One of the greatest joys is the kitchen garden, which leads off the terrace, up steps flanked by pots of scented geraniums and beneath an arch entwined with clematis and wisteria. The vegetable garden, too, has been designed on strong architectural lines, with four box-edged  beds divided by gravel paths. Each bed has a different colour scheme, like a glorious living patchwork. Pinks, blues and mauves are concentrated on the side nearest the house, with bright pink poppies, crimson cactus dahlias and the starry blue flowers of borage among the purple sage and salad greens, while on the far side, nasturtiums in

every shade from deep red through to ochre and lemon romp through beds of zucchini and different varieties of tomatoes. Taller plants such as hollyhocks and globe artichokes provide a change in height. I like to try new varieties of vegetables – yellow beetroots, black plum tomatoes or striped zucchini. Growing flowers amongst the vegetables not only looks good, it also attracts beneficial insects to aid pollination. I love the satisfying geometry of neat lines of crops, with flowers weaving in and out in picturesque abandon. So many people hide their vegetable patches away behind a fence or wall, when they can be such an attractive and enjoyable part of the garden. To me, few things are as pleasurable as wandering among the beds and rows, selecting ripe vegetables for supper, picking the odd sprig of herbs and cutting flowers for the table. It keeps one in tune with the seasons – the excitement of the new growth in spring, the first crops, the abundance of the summer harvest and that slight sadness as autumn ripens into winter – but then the whole cycle begins again.

KEEP IT SIMPLE

Sometimes the simplest things are the best. Freshly baked bread flavoured with rosemary, a garden-grown salad of young leaves, herbs and purple pansies and a delicious homemade plum tart make a summer lunch that is as much a treat for the eye as for the tastebuds.

HYDRANGEAS

Blue has always been a favourite colour. The right shade can provide a soothing backdrop in a sitting room or bedroom. Here a subtle mixture of blues and mauves runs throughout the selection of floral, striped and plain fabrics, the simple flower arrangements and accessories.

ANOTHER SIDE OF INDIA

The colourful side of India is dazzling and always inspiring – the rituals, the textiles, the way flowers are used – but what one never expects is the cool calmness that also coexists there.

I took this photograph early one morning on the beach in Kerala, in the south of India, when the fishing boats were coming in, before the noise and hussle of the day had begun. There is something so serene about it, so absolutely beautiful; it seemed to sum up for me that other side of India – the quiet, contemplative side that can so easily be overlooked.

THE SAMODE PALACE

Every room, every wall, every architrave of the Samode Palace in Rajasthan is covered with these exquisite paintings in blue, white, indigo and turquoise. It is incredible to find all this inspiration and wonderful architecture in one place; a quality of workmanship and devotion to detail that belongs to a way of life that is special and rare.

Inspiration from the colours of India: blue-green gloss paint, pink silk saris, floral offerings in temples and white minarets against clear blue skies

Somehow, these fragments of memory, snatched photographs and scribbles in notebooks find their way into fabric and wallpaper designs.

SCATTERED PETALS

Flowers don't have to be arranged to be appreciated. These tulip heads and petals – simply scattered on a transparent perspex table designed by Danielle Roberts – reveal their hidden inner beauty in a way similar to that captured by Georgia O'Keeffe in her unique paintings.

BLACKBURN COLLEGE LIBRARY

COLLECTING
CONTEMPORARY ART

Q What kind of art do you collect?

At home I have a very eclectic mixture of paintings and prints, all of which have personal meaning. Howard Hodgkin (below right) has been described as 'Britain's greatest living colourist'. He has a highly refined understanding of colour, and his paintings are sensitive, intelligent and extremely emotional – moments in life, or nuances in relationships, captured in pure swirling colour.

Victor Pasmore (top right) Hodgkin's senior but working at the same time, trod a similarly elusive line between observed realism and painterly abstraction, though his canvases tend to be sparser and more cerebral in character.

Bill Jacklin (large painting, left) moved from abstraction in the 1960s to a contemporary form of realistic representation that says as much about the artist's own inner world as about the objects or people he paints. His paintings always have an underlying sense of stillness.

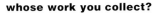

I respond to the meditative character of Craigie Aitchison's work (below left). His canvases of concentrated colour have a tremendous power to move the emotions; I love the impact of one of his small paintings on an expanse of blue wall.

Q Are there similarities between the artists whose work you collect?

The artists you see here are mostly British artists, all of whom are brilliant colourists – which rather negates the often-held view that the British don't use colour. Some are people that I have worked with: Howard Hodgkin, Bill Jacklin and Michael Heindorff have all created fabric designs for Designers Guild.

There is a long tradition of artists collaborating on textiles – Dufy worked on the most wonderful fabrics, as did the Surrealists and many of the Bauhaus artists.

This is an area in which I would definitely like to continue working.

I also have a strong response to the sculptor Barbara Hepworth and her quiet, minimal forms, as well as to Matisse's simple line drawings.

Q The works of art on these and the following pages are shown in your own home, aren't they?

Yes. Everyone has favourite paintings in museums, that can be revisited as a constant source of inspiration over the years. But you have a particular relationship with works of art that you own. Living with works of art – in my case mainly by artists who I know and have worked with – feels different.

The paintings or prints become an accompaniment to life – you live with them in your home, alongside your flowers, your pieces of furniture, and they knit themselves into the fabric of your living space.

HOWARD HODGKIN

"... the exhilarating freedom, boiling colour and charged emotion that we think of as typically Hodgkin." His paintings may often appear to be abstract, but Hodgkin describes himself as "a representational painter of emotional situations".

CRAIGIE AITCHISON

He "distils the everyday into images of poetic economy and beauty".
"His simple, economical, yet profoundly poetical compositions share...
a soothing peacefulness, a palpable mood of silent contemplation."

ART OF THE THEATRE

Theatre design is all about creating atmosphere. David Hockney's opera sets are a wonderful combination of art and theatre. Of course, there is a long tradition of artists designing for the theatre, from Inigo Jones's masques in the 17th century through to Kandinsky's collaboration with Stravinsky's 'Firebird Suite' and Barbara Hepworth's designs for Michael Tippett's 'Midsummer Marriage'. Howard Hodgkin, Sidney Nolan and Georges Rouault have all designed extensively for the opera and ballet, but few artists have done so more than Hockney, who must have a real understanding and love of the music; it obviously inspires him hugely. His sets are very innovative – those for 'The Rake's Progress' and 'The Magic Flute' at Glyndebourne in the 1970s, or Stravinsky's 'Rite of Spring' at the Metropolitan Opera House in New York spring to mind. He also designed sets for Puccini's 'Turandot' and works by Satie, Poulenc and Ravel.

There is something tremendously exciting about the notion of artists moving across disciplines: think of Picasso's spirited ceramics and Matisse's illustrations for Mallarme and James Joyce, and his stained glass, vestments and liturgical objects for the chapel at Vence.

For any creative person, going to a live performance of any of the arts can contribute to the creative process. I believe it brings one's own level of consciousness to a finer place – helps bring one to a state that is quieter and more open. And it is into that state of quietness and openness that ideas and inspiration come.

Being a spectator at the theatre or opera or ballet is something that I find very inspiring. It's enriching on so many levels. You can learn something, you can be dazzled visually, it can touch your heart: how extraordinary is that? I always find the design – the sets and costumes and the entire visual side of the performance – incredibly stimulating. This image sums up the excitement and sheer exuberance of being present at a live performance.

OPERA

THEATRE

SETS

COSTUMES

SPECTACLE

DRAMA

CATWALK

FASHION

Fashion is a demanding and stimulating area of design – the time span is very short, so it often gets dismissed as fickle, but the creative energy and passion involved go far beyond vanity. Designers such as John Galliano and Miuccia Prada take clothes to a higher level – the Prada store in New York, designed by Rem Koolhaas in 2001, is almost like a museum, bringing fashion, art and architecture together in an unprecedented and stimulating way. Christina Kim, of Dosa, has a wonderful sense of colour and travels the world to find beautiful textiles that have a lasting quality, like the lace top pictured opposite.

The history and culture of fashion is fascinating: costume holds strong clues as to what was happening in any era – the status of women, the economy, the spirit of the times. The fabric collections in the Victoria & Albert Museum in London are a great place to explore. Fashion and dress in other societies are so revealing. India is full of extraordinary textiles to treasure, yet in many Indian cities women have stopped wearing saris. The ritualistic approach to dress, as exemplified in old Japanese society, for instance, is something we in the West have almost completely lost – how many women wear hats these days?

Dressing oneself is just another aspect of everyday creativity, and fashion touches everyone in this way. We dress ourselves every morning, and we make these personal and creative decisions every day, whether consciously or not.

1950s FASHION PHOTOGRAPHY

Q What is it about 1950s fashion photography that inspires you?

It's that strong graphic quality, that poise and elegance, which have seldom been surpassed. Modern fashion photography is still an extremely creative field, but it was during the 1950s that images such as those on this and the following pages began to elevate it to an art form.

Q Who is your favourite fashion photographer of that period?

To my mind, few photographers of the period were more talented than Louise Dahl-Wolfe. Richard Avedon summed it up when he said that "the credit line Louise Dahl-Wolfe was the definition of elegance and beauty".

Q Who was Louise Dahl-Wolfe?

She was an American photographer who worked mainly in fashion between the 1930s and the late 1950s, and contributed to the huge success of *Harper's Bazaar* magazine during the era of editor-in-chief Carmel Snow and the famous fashion editor Diana

Vreeland. She pioneered a more relaxed style of American fashion photography – using natural lighting, outdoor settings and unexpected poses – at a time when European fashion was still stuck in a much more stiff and formal mode. Diana Vreeland said of her, "Louise was passionate, more ignited by her métier than anyone I have ever known. She was a great experimenter… a pioneer in colour and daylight."

Q How did her work differ from earlier fashion photography?

She was more like an artist in the way that she worked , declaring "I believe that the camera is a medium of light, that one actually paints with light." She really understood black and white, using all the shades between black and white as colours, so that all the subtle tones have degrees of light and shade in them. Everything she photographed she gave amazing silhouettes and graphic shapes. Her work is never fussy, never over-decorated; it has many of the qualities of good sculpture. This famous picture (left),

'Twins on the Beach', taken in 1955, sums up everything about her work that I admire.

Q Did she have a wider influence beyond fashion?

Oh yes, her portraits of Christopher Isherwood, Jean Cocteau, Collette, Edith Sitwell, Orson Welles and Bette Davis are classics. And her early documentary work photographing Tennessee mountain people in the 1930s was included in the first great world photography exhibition at the Museum of Modern Art. She had a huge influence on Horst, Avedon, Penn and other great American photographers who followed her.

Q What do you think Louise Dahl-Wolfe has to tell us today?

Her work has integrity. She thought all photographers should go to art school, to learn how to look. And she never compromised – when the editorship of *Harper's Bazaar* changed in the late 1950s she realized that the era of true freedom in fashion photography had ended, so she decided to give up fashion photography.

SCHIAPARELLI A TRUE ORIGINAL

The fashion designer Elsa Schiaparelli did far more than famously invent a supposedly 'shocking' shade of pink. As far back as the 1930s, her designs included culottes, padded shoulders and hats shaped like shoes or lamb chops, and she also pioneered the use of zips and synthetic fabrics. Her witty take on fashion had much in common with the Surrealists, with whom she socialized and collaborated – Man Ray, Cocteau, Dali and Dufy were among the artists who designed fabrics for her, and her salon boasted a freestanding ashtray by Giacometti. Schiaparelli also helped to establish the notion of fashion designer as superstar, reaping huge profits from ready-to-wear, perfume and licensing agreements, and using celebrities and film stars to promote her designs.

As a personality, she was as outspoken and daring as her clothes, stating that "Fashion is born by small facts, trends or even politics, never by trying to make little pleats and furbelows, by trinkets, by clothes easy to copy or by the shortening or lengthening of a skirt... In difficult times fashion is always outrageous."

"Women dress alike all over the world: they dress to be annoying to other women."

Elsa Schiaparelli

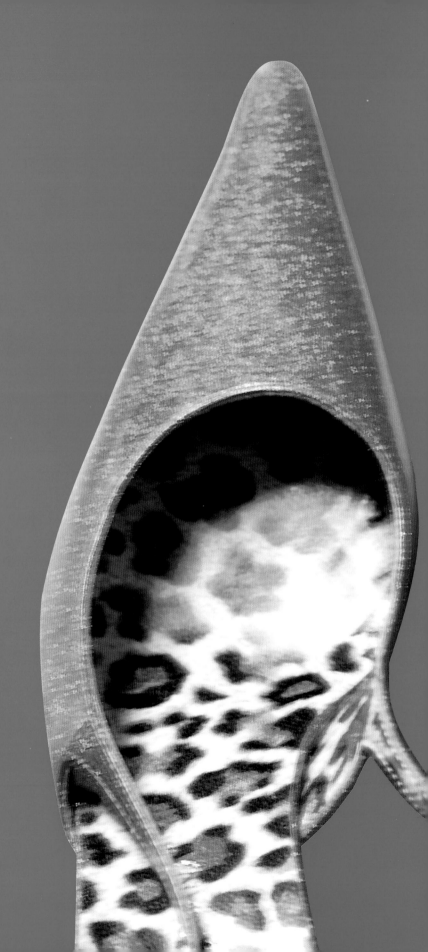

GREAT SHOES

ARCHITECTURAL ORIGINALITY

This display stand for the Marni shop in London is a perfect fusion of architecture, design and fashion. Marni clothes are all about freedom of spirit, pattern and form, and Future Systems display similar qualities in their architecture. With this wonderfully graphic curve they have created a completely new way of displaying clothes.

FEATHERS
IRIDESCENCE

The iridescent qualities of feathers in the natural world are imitated in textiles by silk – look at the way the colours and textures of the cushions in this room relate and react to the light. They are brought alive by the contrast with the matt texture of the wall behind, and by the fact that there is a lot of white in the room. It's all about the relationship between things – in this case between the shiny and the matt, the colour and the white background, between objects and space.

MARC QUINN

British artist Marc Quinn freezes real flowers – that could never conceivably grow together in a garden – in a glass case, perpetuating their fresh, fleshy beauty, but adding a subtly sinister note.

EARLY ITALIAN FRESCOS

Work by the early Italian artists who painted churches – among them Giotto, Masaccio, Piero della Francesca and Perugino – still has the power to transmit to us the spiritual nature of the task in which they were involved: they were telling stories from the Bible, as well as expressing themselves artistically. Their work has a timelessness that transcends the centuries. Immerse yourself in some of the details of Giotto's frescos at the Basilica of St Francis in Assisi and the forms and colours look completely modern. Their resonance remains in the mind and memory for many years to come and can be an unexpected source of inspiration. Years afterwards, you can come across that same shade of remembered blue – in the petals of a flower, or the light on the water of a swimming pool.

The early Renaissance artists also used aspects of their own daily life and surroundings in their paintings, which still speak strongly to us in the 21st century. Look at the heads of Piero della Francesca's madonnas: you still see women with that beautiful wide bone structure in Tuscany and Umbria today. And the countryside he painted as the backdrop to many of his works remains unchanged and recognizable as the hills and cypress trees around the town of his birth.

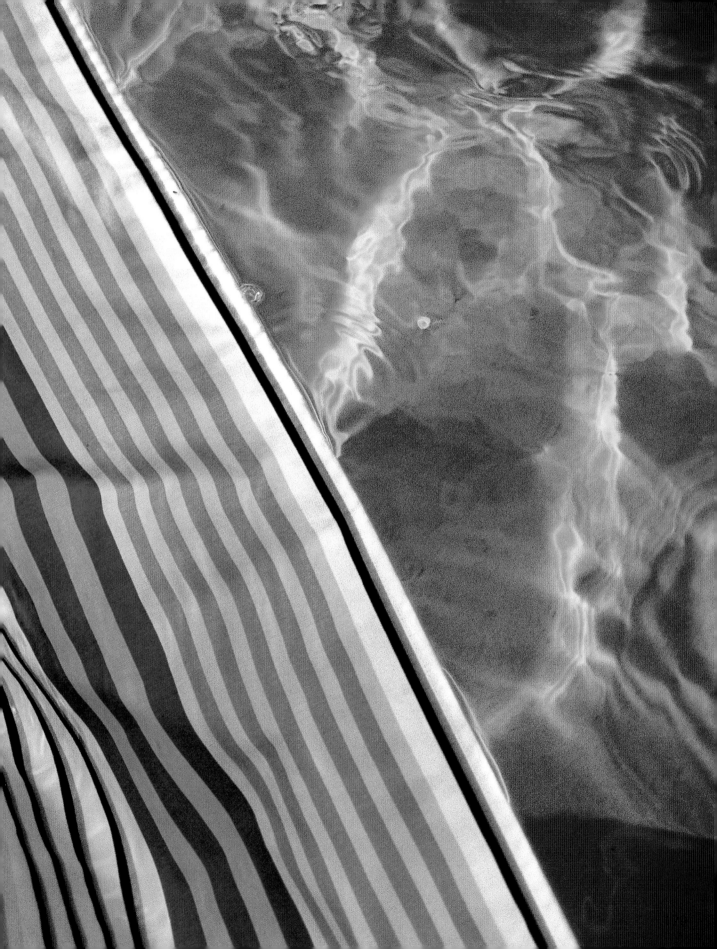

VENICE

Venice has attracted artists throughout its history and, like the Taj Mahal, is one of those places that seem almost too obvious, too well known, to be inspirational. And yet, in spite of us knowing them so well from having seen so many images, in reality they never fail to surprise. Everything about Venice is extraordinary, from the buildings to its history to the water buses and the whole way of life there. It's easy to understand why it has inspired so many artists and writers throughout history. So many images remain in my mind, from a tiny fragment of a mosaic in St Mark's Square to Veronese's frescos of Saint Sebastian, and from the colour and life of the fish market to the visual poetry of the gondola posts. I keep on going back there, visiting my favourite churches, buying handmade glass and papers, getting lost as I explore the back streets. Something in me feels that I have to capture it; I can't believe the place is still standing, that the way of life has also survived.

PALLADIO AND VERONESE

What I find astonishing about Palladio's 16th-century villas in the valley of the Veneto in northern Italy is their sense of proportion, and the way in which the painted decorations fit so seamlessly with the simple, almost austere elegance of the architecture. When you walk into buildings such as the Villa Barbaro at Maser you are immediately affected by their quiet beauty.

Artists such as Veronese and Tiepolo were commissioned to paint series of frescos on the walls and, having been so used to working in churches, one can sense their feeling of freedom in being able to paint scenes from daily life, portraits of the inhabitants, the details of contemporary costume. Looking at them today, there is a real modernity about them – a strong graphic quality accompanied by a touching softness that means they are never overpowering. In this detail of one of the vaulted ceilings of the Villa Barbaro, frescoed by Veronese, a young boy holding a book leans over the trompe-l'oeil balustrade.

The fabrics on the following pages feature a combination of colours which, if not inspired directly by this particular image, owe a lot to the essence, or spirit, of these frescos. These are quite heavy, rich neutral colours, and yet there is a lightness about the figure that draws the eye. This lightness is something I have tried to emulate when using similar colours in the room overleaf – by combining the dark browns and neutrals with lots of white and light contemporary furniture the mood is balanced, and not overtly masculine, as could so often be the result when using this palette.

PORCELAIN

The delightful, delicate fragility of antique and modern porcelain... The intricate forms and handpainted flowers on this eclectic collection of pieces – all fragments from larger tea sets and services that have been broken, dispersed or forgotten – provided inspiration for a modern use of pale pastel colours (see overleaf).

Inspired by the pale pastels and delicate forms of Sevres porcelain, this interior is suffused with light, modern romance. The palest pink of the low linen sofa anchors the scheme, with a pale painted floor, slightly darker pinks for the armchairs, embroidered cushions and simple posies of pale pink roses. The striped cushions and bright camellia print at the windows add a bold modern note that banishes any suggestions of sentimentality.

SWEET THINGS

Scoops of ice cream, curls of chocolate, crisp pink linen and sprigs of the first cherry blossom…

AMALFI COASTLINE

From the ancient gardens of Ravello, the brightly painted houses and terraces of lemon groves clinging to the mountainous coastline, to the glorious cathedral in Amalfi, this seminal landscape has attracted writers, composers, artists and poets for centuries.

PRETTY FL

LAMINGOS

MY FAIR LADY

Black and white with a touch of
pink… Fortnum & Mason hatboxes…
Cecil Beaton's *fin de siecle* designs…
Audrey Hepburn's perfect poise in
that supremely elegant costume…
a shorthand for pure style…
a distillation of elegance…

People always ask where inspiration comes
from, and you don't always know, but in this
room I was looking for that same feeling of
timeless elegance displayed by those
wonderful Cecil Beaton costumes.

MODERN FURNITURE

Modern furniture is a major component in my design philosophy: it runs right through this book and through all my work. The pieces I select for the rooms we create are usually a mix of Designers Guild furniture and the work of various 20th- and 21st-century designers. There is such a rich choice – from classics by

Arne Jacobsen, Eero Saarinen and Verner Panton (which still seem so startlingly modern that it is hard to believe they are decades old).

There are a number of designers whose work I use constantly. Ron Arad's furniture combines an element of humour with tremendously clever design: his red 'Fantastic Elastic' chair (left) and 'Tom Vac' scoop of white plastic (centre right) are good illustrations of his unconventional approach to materials. Philippe Starck's ultra-stylish, pared-down modernism has a lightness of

touch that is always recognizable and instantly covetable, and he never forgets about comfort. Jasper Morrison's low leather sofas and arm chairs have a timeless appeal that works in almost any interior, and Tom Dixon is another favourite – I have lived with his famous S chair for many years. Innovative companies such as

Cappellini, B&B Italia and Driade work with major designers and architects to make beautiful furniture available to everyone. Other good examples include Patrick Norguet's funky striped Perspex Rainbow chair, brought out in 2000 (top right) and Karim Rashid's Butterfly chair (bottom left).

The best modern furniture design embraces shape, form and colour. Sometimes the forms alone are splendidly sculptural and can hold a space in their own right. With other pieces the appeal is mainly one of comfort. Playing with different upholstery fabrics can transform a simple shape: the Barber Osgobie

'Superlight' sofa (far left and opposite) looks cool and contemporary in pale green washed linen, but using pink striped velvet or a bold print would put a completely new spin on it. This can be a great way to personalize the designs of furniture you own and make them your own.

Furniture takes on a different character according to its surroundings: the pieces shown opposite would appear very different in an old French château or in a huge modern loft. As it is, they have been photographed in my study at home – a space that is characterized by the quality of light that pours through the floor-to-ceiling doors and windows and the slices of glass that have been

added as sky lights in the roof. Look at the shine on Ron Arad's red chair and Lena Bergstrom's glass bowl. In this scheme the strong individual elements are held together by the modern black-and-white striped rug.

My desk ready for work: a contemporary etched glass table and a white Tulip chair by Eero Saarinen from the 1950s, upholstered in one of our retro-inspired fabrics. Inspirational objects are close at hand – fresh flowers, old and new textiles, favourite books and pictures. A freshly made cappuccino completes the scene.

True minimalism: a brushed metal Philippe Starck table, moulded plastic Verner Panton chairs and the most pared-down of flower arrangements: single white amaryllis stems in slim black and white vases.

This clean white modern space was a wonderful blank canvas for modern furniture and fabrics – glazed walls leading on to a well-kept garden. The banners of fabric are simple sliding blinds that can be moved about depending on where the sun is, but they are as bold as a modern painting. This contemporary approach to using pattern appears neither old fashioned nor sentimental.

Red upholstery can bring back real or imagined memories of old-fashioned boudoirs and stuffy club furniture. Here, we turned such connotations on their head by using bright red velvet on this modern Balance day bed. The glossy red Eros chair by Philippe Starck adds a further contemporary note, while crumpled silk curtains, crimson peonies and a single orange poppy contribute a touch of romance in tune with the white wedding-cake mouldings on the walls.

ARNE JACOBSEN

Q Don't the chairs in this period photograph look modern?

Jacobsen's designs still look so contemporary today that we forget that he was designing as early as the 1930s and 1940s. This picture shows the foyer of a very impressive hotel in Copenhagen that he designed in the late 1950s. Because his furniture design has been his lasting legacy, it is not now widely known that he was also a very successful architect in his day. The Royal Hotel is well worth a visit – the interiors have been perfectly preserved and it is extraordinary how modern it still looks.

For this project Jacobsen designed the Swan chair and matching Swan sofa, to be upholstered in purple wool, and the equally famous Egg chair with its sensual cocooning shape. The shapes are organic, like abstract sculpture, and there is a timelessness that makes this furniture as desirable now as it was when it was first made.

Q What are Jacobsen's other best-known designs?

His stackable Ant and Series 7 chairs, with their moulded one-piece plywood seat and back and tubular steel legs, were produced in 1952 and 1955 and have been in continuous production ever since. We sell them in the Designers Guild Homestore in modern shades of bright pink, purple and lime green.

Q What about his other designs?

Jacobsen's architecture was very restrained and minimalist – the perfect setting for his furniture. He designed St Catherine's College, Oxford, in 1962, which is now a Grade I listed building and was one of his own favourite pieces of work. On a smaller scale, he also applied his talents to light fittings, cutlery and ceramics. His teapot, coffee jug, milk jug and tea strainer were recently re-issued in honour of the centenary of his birth.

Q Why do you think his designs have lasted so well?

I think it's the fusion of innovative ideas with technical expertise. The construction of everything he designed is so good. Jacobsen worked closely with manufacturers in a way that Italian industrial designers were also doing at the time. The furniture designs in particular combine minimalism with elegance and comfort. On another level, they relate to the city spaces that many young people live in today – the Swan and Egg chairs look fabulous in modern lofts and city apartments and the stacking chairs are practical as well as stylish for small urban spaces.

Here is Jacobsen's Swan chair nearly half a century on, in this case upholstered in black leather and looking absolutely contemporary in a modern interior. It has all the impact of a piece of modern sculpture and the black sets off the form, highlighting the contrast of all those voluptuous curves with the stripes on the fabric and the straight lines of the architecture. We had fun creating a lively eclectic mixture of contemporary and retro – a retro-inspired print in bright colours for the curtains, handmade modern vessels on the table, modern furniture that nods to the low, languid shapes of the 1970s, a round Tulip table designed in the 1950s by Jacobsen's contemporary Eero Saarinen, and a quirky lamp from the same period. It's hard to imagine any of Jacobsen's designs looking anything other than modern

CHINA ROSE

Think of roses and your mind usually fills with images of country flowers, the great English rose gardens, and traditional chintzy fabrics. Here, however, roses are used in a modern and completely un-nostalgic way. The fabric design has been painted in a very graphic contemporary way that makes the flowers glamorous rather than country, especially when coupled with the luxurious silks and velvets used elsewhere in the room. This is what I'm always aiming for in my work. I might get inspiration from nature or from old documents, but will always try to take it in a new direction, so that the finished design is very much of the present. Despite its contemporary feel, it still looks absolutely at home with traditional architecture, with antique furniture and with old crystal chandeliers.

COCKTAIL HOUR

A quirky contemporary mix of different cocktail glasses, sweetheart biscuits, fruit and flowers in bright berry colours.

MODERN ROMANCE

Fresh flowers bring light and romance to a room; without them the space feels dead and uninhabited. The more fragile and ephemeral the blooms, the more closely they connect us to the eternal cycle of life.

The camellia is another flower that has old-fashioned connotations. But these painterly yet graphic images in shades of red, pink and white bring an air of modern romance to this contemporary interior, making a striking mix with the bold stripes on the sofa, the low leather Jasper Morrison chairs and the shiny white lacquered table designed by MDF Italia.

PICTURE ACKNOWLEDGMENTS

The list below includes information about the paintings and photographs included in the book, as well as acknowledgments and thanks to all those who have given their kind permission for the use of their images in this book.

All photographs not listed below are © James Merrell

Pages 2-3 Pansy butterfly © Gettyimages/Geoff du Feu

7 Butterfly © Tophampicturepoint

8-9 Paintings by Henri Matisse. **8** *Coucous sur le Tapis Bleu et Rose,* by Henri Matisse (1911), © Bridgeman Art Library/Christie's Images, London, UK/© Succession H. Matisse/DACS 2004. **9** (above) *Seville Still Life,* by Henri Matisse (1910), © Bridgeman Art Library/© Succession H. Matisse/DACS 2004; (centre) *Harmony in Red,* by Henri Matisse (1908) © The Art Archive/Hermitage Museum Saint Petersburg/Album/Joseph Martin/© Succession H. Matisse/DACS 2004; (below) *The Lagoon,* plate XVIII from "Jazz," by Henri Matisse (1947), © Bridgeman Art Library/The Stapleton Collection/© Succession H. Matisse/DACS 2004

11 All Caribbean photographs by Tricia Guild except (below centre) Dahlia 'Madeline's Aloha' © Garden Picture Library/J.S. Sira

12-3 Goldfish © Gettyimages/Peter Scoones

20-1 All India photographs by Tricia Guild except 20 (above right) *The Young Mughal Emperor Muhammad Shah at a Nautch Performance* (c. 1725), © Bridgeman Art Library/Victoria & Albert Museum, London

28 Cherry blossom © Garden Picture Library

29 Geishas Geiko-san and Maiko-san walking under cherry blossom, Kyoto, Japan (1999), © Magnum/Chris Steele-Perkins

30-1 Paris. **30** (above left) New craze, tea-dancing in a swimming pool, 1930s © Corbis/Bettmann; (above right) American model kissing French waiter © Corbis/Peter Turnley; (centre left) Gene Kelly and Nina Foch in *An American in Paris* (1951) © Corbis/John Springer Collection; (centre right) Sidewalk cafés on the Champs Elysées © Corbis/Bettmann; (below left) Girl at a bar © Corbis/David Turnley; (below right) Street scene with people sitting in café and promenading down street © Topham Picturepoint. **31** (above left) Couple chatting over drinks © Corbis/Lucien Aigner; (above right) Sitting under umbrella at pavement café © Topham Picturepoint; (centre left) Neon café sign © Corbis/Casa Productions; (centre right) Le Royal St Germain restaurant at night © Topham Picturepoint; (below left) Couple drinking at Paris pavement café © Rex Features/Roger Viollet Archive; (below centre) Model with dogs © Topham Picturepoint; (below right) Three young women walking with arms linked © Rex Features/Roger Viollet Archive

32 Inside the entrance of the Pyramide du Louvre, Paris. Architect I.M. Pei, Pei Cobb Freed & Partners © Corbis/Bernard Bisson

33 Two tourists under an archway looking at architect I M Pei, Pei Cobb Freed & Partners' Louvre Pyramid © Corbis/Nathan Benn

34-5 Topiary in the gardens at Levens Hall, Cumbria, England © Garden Picture Library/Clive Boursnell

36-7 The gardens at Levens Hall, Cumbria, England. **36** (left) © Andrew Lawson; (centre & right) © Marianne Majerus. **37** (left) © Andrew Lawson; (centre) © Garden Picture Library/Linda Burgess; (right) © Marianne Majerus

38-9 Guggenheim Museum, Bilbao, Spain, architect Frank O. Gehry. **38** © Artur/Jochen Helle.
39 © Impact Photos/R Roberts

40 Barbara Hepworth working on *Sphere and the Inner Form,* in her studio in St Ives, 1963 © Topham Picturepoint

42-3 Red car in Cuba © Photolibrary.com/Gair Photographic Dan. **43** Aqua car in Cuba © Gettyimages/Geoff Turner

44-5 Houses designed by Luis Barragan. **44** Multi-image of stable, house, pool and horse in San Cristobal, Mexico City © Magnum/René Burri. **45** (above right) Casa Gilardin, Mexico City © Undine Pröhl; (centre & below right) Detail of house and garden in San Cristobal, Mexico City © Magnum/René Burri

46 *Dama de Blano,* by Frida Kahlo (1928) © 2004 Banco de México Diego Rivera & Frida Kahlo Museums Trust, Av. Cinco de Mayo No. 2, Col. Centro, Del. Cuauhtémoc 06059, México. D.F./Bridgeman Art Library

47 (above) Garden of Frida Kahlo and Diego Rivera's house in Mexico © Tim Street-Porter; (centre) Portrait of Frida Kahlo (1910-1954) taken in 1944 © Corbis/Bettmann; (below) Interior of Frida Kahlo and Diego Rivera's house in Mexico © Tim Street-Porter

48-9 Modern ceramics. **48** (left) Rosaria Rattan for Kose and (right) Liz Hodges. **49** (top right) Liz Hodges; (top left) Linda Hoffhines; (centre right) Janice Tchalenko; (bottom left) Carol McNicholl; (bottom right) Linda Hoffhines.

50-1 Porcelain by Liz Hodges, Kose and Sandy Dwyer.

52-3 Glass vase by Memphis.

54-5 54 (top shelf) and **55** Bruce McLean. **54** (lower shelf) striped pot and red pot by Henriette Gaillard.

56-7 Detail of Paper Kite butterfly wing © Gettyimages/George Lepp

60-3 Photographs by James Merrell © House & Garden/The Condé Nast Publications Ltd.

66-8 Guanock House garden designed by Arne Maynard Garden Design. Photographs by Rosie Atkins.

74-5 Photographs by Tricia Guild

76-7 Outdoor Living. All photographs by James Merrell except those with striped fabric (76 centre and 77 top left) by Tricia Guild.

80-1 Photographs by Tricia Guild.

84-5 Photographs by Tricia Guild.

88-9 All India photographs by Tricia Guild.

94 Large painting by Bill Jacklin. **95** Paintings by (top right) Victor Pasmore; (centre) *A Swan StillLife* by Craigie Aitchison; (bottom) *You and Me* by Howard Hodgkin

96-7 Painting by Howard Hodgkin

98-9 *Crucifixion* by Craigie Aitchison

100-1 Details of large-scale painted environments with separate elements based on Hockney's designs (1983) for Stravinsky's Opera, *The Rake's Progress.* **100** "Auction Scene" Ink, charcoal on canvas and laminated foamboard. 120 x 192 x 192" © David Hockney. **101** "Bedlam". Ink, acrylic on plaster, wood and cloth. 120 x 192 x 192" © David Hockney/photographed by James Franklin

102-3 Dancer at Beijing Opera, © Gettyimages/Bob Handelman

104-5 Pink dress designed by John Galliano for the Christian Dior Autumn/Winter 2003/4 collection, © Camera Press

108 *Twins on the Beach* by Louise Dahl-Wolfe, © Louise Dahl-Wolfe/Courtesy Staley-Wise Gallery, New York

110 (left) Model wearing button-back skirt and sealskin slip-cover cape, with gloves and handbag, all by Balmain (1955) © Corbis/Condé Nast Archive/photographed by Henry Clarke; (centre) Mrs. Marion Hargrove at the steering wheel of a convertible, wearing a linen town dress with a black bow and a cashmere sweater over her shoulders (1954) © Corbis/Condé

Nast Archive/photographed by Leombruno-Bodi; (right) Model wearing black dress and white hat by Hattie Carnegie, with white bowknot satin sleeves by Balenciaga (1953) © Corbis/Condé Nast Archive/ photographed by John Rawlings

111 (left) Model in front of London store window, wearing tweed sheath coat dress and hat, both by Dior (1955) © Corbis/Condé Nast Archive/ photographed by Henry Clarke; (centre) Model wearing Balenciaga tweed dress with double-breasted skirt, fur ascot, hat, and gloves, holding circular handbag (1955) © Corbis/Condé Nast Archive/ photographed by Henry Clarke; (right) Woman modelling black velvet visor with rhinestone pin and satin scarf, both by Dior, (1952) © Corbis/Condé Nast Archive/photographed by Henry Clarke

112-3 Designs by Elsa Schiaparelli. **112** Model with her back to camera sitting on arm of chair in dress designed by Elsa Schiaparelli, photograph by Horst P. Horst, © Horst/*Vogue* © 1947 Condé Nast Publications. 113 Portrait of Elsa Schiaparelli by Horst P. Horst, © Horst/*Vogue* © 1937 Condé Nast Publications

114-5 Pink shoes © Photonica/Bill Diodata

116-7 The Marni shop in Sloane Street, designed by Future Systems © Richard Davies

118-9 and 121 (centre) Close-up of Macaw feathers © Corbis/George D. Lepp

119 Pair of budgerigars © Gettyimages/Chris Warbey

122-3 *Italian Landscape* (12) by Marc Quinn, 2000 (permanent pigment on canvas) © Marc Quinn, courtesy Jay Jopling/White Cube (London)

124-5 Detail of the angel from *The Vision of the Throne* (A throne destined for St Francis appears to the monk Pacificus; Legenda maior VI, 6) by Giotto di Bondone. Fresco c. 1295/1300. Assisi, S. Francesco (Upper church, nave, 2nd bay, north wall). © AKG akg-images/Stefan Diller.

126-7 Detail of the flock from *Stories of Gioacchino & Anna: I dream of Gioacchio* by Giotto di Bondone. Fresco c. 1304-1306 Padua, Cappella degli Scrovegni, © Photoservice Electa, Milano courtesy of Ministero per I Beni e le Attività Culturali

128-9 Photograph by Tricia Guild.

130-1 (above) Detail from gold mosaic at St Mark's Cathedral, Venice, © AKG/Erich Lessing; (below) Gondolas on the Grand Canal, Venice, © John Heseltine

132-3 Detail of a man reading from the *Fresco and Stucco Cycle at Villa Barbaro* by Veronese and Alessandro Vittoria, © Corbis/Araldo de Luca

144-5 The Amalfi coastline. **144** (left) Sunbathers on the beach © Topham Picturepoint; (centre) Boats on the beach © Photolibrary.com; (right) Amalfi harbour, Gulf of Salerno © Corbis/Vittoriano Rastelli. **145** (far left) © Magnum/Martin Parr; (left) Fishing boats, Amalfi © Corbis/Richard T. Nowitz; (right) Man painting in street © Topham Picturepoint; (far right) Beach umbrellas, Positano © Corbis/Jonathan Blair

146-7 Greater flamingoes in Africa © Gettyimages/John Giustina

148 and 149 Audrey Hepburn as Eliza Doolittle in *My Fair Lady,* courtesy of The Kobal Collection/Warner Bros

153 (top right) Rainbow chair by Capellini

164-5 Swan chairs designed by Arne Jacobsen in the lobby of Hotel Royal, 30 August 1963, and detail, © Topham Picturepoint/Polfoto

Every effort has been made at the time of going to press to trace the copyright holders, architects and designers whose work appears in this book. We apologise for any unintentional omission and would be pleased to insert the appropriate acknowledgement in any subsequent edition.

DESIGNERS GUILD STOCKISTS

Designers Guild fabric, wallpaper, furniture and accessories are available from:

Designers Guild
Showroom and Homestore
267-277 Kings Road
London SW3 5EN
tel 020 7351 5775

and from selected retailers including:

bath & n.e.somerset
BRISTOL GUILD OF APPLIED ART
68-70 Park Street Bristol BS1 5JY
0117 926 5548
JANE CLAYTON AND COMPANY
Unit 12 Old Mills Paulton Bristol
BS39 7SU 01761 412255
ROSSITERS OF BATH
38-41 Broad Street Bath BA1 5LP
01225 462227

berkshire
JACQELINE INTERIORS
18 Brockenhurst Road South Ascot
SL5 9DL 01344 638867

buckinghamshire
JOHN LEWIS FURNISHINGS & LEISURE
Holmers Farm Way Cressex Centre
High Wycombe HP12 4NW
01494 462666
MORGAN GILDER FURNISHINGS
14 High Street Stony Stratford
Milton Keynes MK11 1AF 01908 568674

cambridgeshire
AT HOME
44 Newnham Road Cambridge CB3 9EY
01223 321283

cheshire
JOHN LEWIS
Wilmslow Road Cheadle SK8 3BZ
01614 914914
ROSI INTERIORS
45 Oxford Road Altrincham WA14 2DY
0161 929 9780

essex
ASPECTS INTERIORS LTD
Unit 1 Nags Corner Winston Rd Nayland
Colchester C06 4LT 01206 262 666
CLEMENT JOSCELYNE
9-11 High Street Brentwood CM14 4RG
01277 225420
COSTELLO LIFESTYLE
45 Sir Isaacs Walk Colchester CO1 1JJ
01206 575159
DEVON HOUSE INTERIORS
3-5 Devon House Hermon Hill
Wanstead E11 2AW 020 8518 8112
KRYSIA
24 Baddow Road Chelmsford CM2 0DG
01245 250856
LOTTIE MUTTON
45 King Street Saffron Walden CB11 1EU
01799 522 252
PAYTON INTERIORS LTD
Bretts Farm Market Chelmsford Road
White Roding CM6 1RF 01279 876 867

gloucestershire
UPSTAIRS DOWNSTAIRS
19 Rotunda Terrace Montpellier Street
Cheltenham GL50 1SW 01242 514023

hampshire
THE INTERIOR TRADING CO
55-57 Marmion Road Southsea PO5 2AT
023 9283 8038

hertfordshire
CLEMENT JOSCELYNE
Market Square Bishop's Stortford
CM23 3XA 01279 713010
CLEMENT JOSCELYNE
111-112 Bancroft Hitchin SG5 1LT
01462 436533
DAVID LISTER INTERIORS
6 Leyton Road Harpenden AL5 2TL
01582 764270
ELIZABETH STEWART
DESIGN & FURNISHING
201-203 High Street Potters Bar EN6 5DA
01707 663433
1 Exchange Buildings High Street Barnet
EN5 5SY 0208 440 6363

ireland
BRIAN S. NOLAN LTD
102 Upper Georges Street Dun Laoghaire
Co Dublin 00 353 1 2800564
J LYONS INTERIORS
Market House The Square Castlerea
Co Roscommon 00 353 90720339
O'MAHONY INTERIORS
Enniskeane West Cork
00 353 2347123

kent
COLOURS ETC. LTD
164 High Street Rochester ME1 1EX
01634 845534
FABRICS IN CANTERBURY
Albert House 14 St Johns Lane Castle
Street Canterbury CT1 2QG
01227 457555
JOHN LEWIS
Bluewater Greenhithe DA9 9SA
01322 624123
KOTIKI INTERIORS LTD
22-24 Grove Hill Road
Tunbridge Wells TN1 1RZ
01892 521369
MARY ENSOR INTERIORS
13 Crescent Road Tunbridge Wells
TN1 2LU 01892 523003
SUNDRIDGE INTERIORS
11-12 Sundridge Parade Plaistow Lane
Sundridge Park Bromley BR1 4DT
020 8466 6313

lancashire
JOHN THOMPSON DESIGN CENTRE
336 Church Street Blackpool FY1 3QH
01253 302515

leicestershire
HARLEQUIN INTERIORS
11 Loseby Lane Leicester LE1 5DR
0116 262 0994
BARKERS INTERIORS
94 Main Street Woodhouse Eaves
Loughborough LE12 8RZ
01509 890473

london
CAMERON BROOM
The Courtyard 15 Bellevue Road
SW17 7EG 020 8767 2241

CHARLES PAGE INTERIORS LTD
61 Fairfax Road NW6 4EE
020 7328 9851
DESIGNERS GUILD
267 & 277 Kings Road SW3 5EN
020 7351 5775
HARRODS
87-135 Brompton Road Knightsbridge
SW1X 7XL 020 7730 1234
HEAL & SON
196 Tottenham Court Road W1P 9LD
020 7636 1666
INTERIORS OF CHISWICK
454 Chiswick High Road W4 5TT
020 8994 0073
JOHN LEWIS
Oxford Street W1A 1EX 020 7629 7711
PETER JONES
Sloane Square SW1W 8EL 020 7730 3434
LIBERTY
Regent Street W1 6AH 020 7734 1234
MR JONES
175-179 Muswell Hill Broadway
Muswell Hill N10 3RS 020 8444 6066
REVAMP INTERIORS
26 Knights Hill West Norwood SE27 0HY
020 8670 5151
SELFRIDGES
Oxford Street W1A 1AB 020 7629 1234

manchester
HEALS
11 New Cathedral Street Manchester
M1 1AD 0161 8193000
ORCHARD INTERIOR DESIGN
2 Warburton Street Didsbury Village
Manchester M20 6WA
0161 434 6278

norfolk
DESIGNERS GUILD AT THE GRANARY
5 Bedford Street Norwich NR2 1AL
01603 623220

northamptonshire
CLASSIX DESIGN & DEVELOPMENT LTD
Billing Wharf Cogenhoe Northampton
NN7 1NH 01604 891333

northern ireland
BEECHGROVE INTERIORS
53a Loan Road Cullybackey Ballymena
Co Antrim BT42 1PS
028 25 880012
FULTONS FINE FURNISHINGS
Hawthorne House Boucher Crescent
Belfast BT12 6HU 0870 600 0186
The Point Derrychara Enniskillen
BT74 6JF 01365 323739
55-63 Queen Street Lurgan
BT66 8BN 01762 314980
PATTONS
Bushmills Road Coleraine BT52 2NU
028 703 52759

nottinghamshire
NASH INTERIORS
60 Derby Road Nottingham NG1 5FD
0115 941 3811

oxfordshire
ANNE HAIMES INTERIORS
27 Duke Street Henley-on-Thames
RG9 1UR 01491 411424

FAIRFAX INTERIORS
The Old Bakery High Street Lower Brailes
Nr Banbury OX15 5HW 01608 685301
STELLA MANNERING LTD
2 Woodstock Road Oxford OX2 6HT
01865 557196

scotland
CAIRNS INTERIORS
111 High Street Old Aberdeen
Aberdeen AB24 3EN 01224 487490
CHELSEA MCLAINE INTERIOR
DESIGN
161 Milngavie Road Bearsden Glasgow
G61 3DY 0141 942 2833
DESIGNWORKS
38 Gibson Street Glasgow G12 8NX
0141 339 9520
JOHN LEWIS
St James Centre Edinburgh EH1 3SP
0131 556 9121
JOHN LEWIS
Buchanan Galleries Glasgow G1 2GF
0141 353 6677
KENSINGTON INTERIORS
109-111 Clarence Drive Glasgow
G12 9RW 0141 338 6798
LAURA GILL DESIGN LTD
38 High Street Dunblane FK15 0AD
01786 821948

somerset
PAUL CARTER
The Studio Elm House Chip Lane
Taunton TA1 1BZ 01823 330404
THE CURTAIN POLE
64 High Street Glastonbury BA6 9DY
01458 834166

suffolk
CLEMENT JOSCELYNE
16 Langton Place Bury St Edmunds
IP33 1NE 01284 753824
EDWARDS OF HADLEIGH
53 High Street Hadleigh 1P7 5AB
01473 827271

surrey
BABAYAN PEARCE INTERIORS
Braeside House High Street Oxshott
KT22 0JP 01372 842437
CHAMELEON
7 High Street Esher KT10 9RL
01372 470 720
CREATIVE INTERIORS
20 Chipstead Station Parade Chipstead
CR5 3TE 01737 555443
DESIGN STUDIO
39 High Street Reigate RH2 9AE
01737 248228
HEAL & SON
Tunsgate Guildford GU1 3QU
01483 576715
HEAL & SON
49-51 Eden Street Kingston upon Thames
KT1 1BW 020 8614 5900
JOHN LEWIS
Wood Street Kingston upon Thames
KT1 1TE 020 8547 3000
J DECOR INTERIORS
3 South Street Epsom KT18 7PJ
01372 721773

©DESIGNERS GUILD™ is a registered trademark of the Designers Guild group of companies

DESIGNERS GUILD REFERENCES

All Designers Guild fabrics, wallpaper and
upholstered furniture are available from
Designers Guild stockists. Other featured
furniture and accessories are available from:

**Designers Guild Homestore
267-277 Kings Road,
London SW3 5EN
tel 020 7351 5775**

Designers Guild products are available worldwide.
For further information please contact:

London 3 Latimer Place London W10 6QT
tel 020 7893 7400 fax 020 7893 7730
info@designersguild.com

Munich tel 01805 244 344 fax 01805 244 345
Paris tel +33 1 44 67 80 70 fax +33 1 44 67 80 71
Milan tel 00 800 1911 2001 fax 00 800 2011 2001
www.designersguild.com

Page 4
Morskaya Aqua Wide Square chair
    F1068/02.
Silk curtains in Pavlosk Schiaperelli
    F1064/01.
Pale blue Coffee Bean table.

Pages 16-7
Fabric panels in Innessa Ocean F1058/03.
Space chair in Trezzini Ocean F1061/01.
Sky chair and stool in chalk leather.
White Mono table by Michael Sodeau.

Page 50
White Ferro dining table. Kose white ceramics.

Pages 58-9
Masuda peat embroidered curtains and bedcover
    F1080/02.
Checked curtains at window Taisha Natural
    F1087/04.
Antique upholstered bench in Jinsha Natural
    F1084/04.
Striped cushion on bed Hakama Slate
    F1082/01.
Red checked cushion on bed Aruna Scarlet
    F1088/03.

Pages 82-3
Lamartine cornflower printed curtains
    F1120/02.
Scroll sofa I Nara chalk F1077/27.
Box chair in Veran sky F1126/06,
    Back cushion in Veran Denim F1126/07.
Asciano blue striped blanket on sofa.

Page 90
Wide Square chair in Bokashi Ocean
    F1083/03.
Cushion in Masuda aqua F1080/04.
Striped cushion in Jinsha Ocean F1084/03.
Embroidered curtain in Nishida Viola F1078/02.
Printed curtain Tsubaki Porcelain F1074/01.

Page 92
Silk curtain in Eugenia Aqua F1104/03.
Danielle Roberts clear Perspex table with
    painted flowers.

Pages 120-1
Flat fabric panel Varya Turquoise F1054/01.
Silk quilt in Pavlosk Mango F1064/11 and Mitia
    Lime F1066/01.
Silk pillows in Amalia Marine F1065/02.
Wall painted in Designers Guild Ocean paint.

Pages 128-9
Striped Bokashi Ocean outdoor fabric
    F1144/03.

Pages 134-5
Curtain in China Rose Ecru F1094/03.
Scoop Sofa in Saraceno Linen F1109/05.
Scoop Chair in Caterina Raven F1101/02.

Pages 138-9
Edge Sofa in Brera Shell F562/27.
Curtains in Mirabeau Rose F1123/02.
Curtains in Eugenia Sand F1104/07.
Edge chairs in Paladru Lilac F1089/24 and
    Brera Cyclamen F562/22.

Pages 150-1
Two Seat Square sofa in Perilla Charcoal
    F1093/05.
Flower print curtain in Colorette Blossom
    F1096/03.
Striped silk curtain and cushion on sofa in
    Francia Graphite F1105/08.

Pages 152-3
Barber Osgobie Superlight sofa in
    Brera Grass Green F562/11.
White oval She Table by David Design.
Cannot Table by Cappellini.
Ron Arad red Fantastic Elastic chair.
Turquoise and lime Butterfly chair by
    Karim Rashid.
Geometric striped Designers Guild rug.

Pages 158-9
Fabric panels in Zinaida Mandarin F1052/02.
Sky Sofa in Rosca Lime F1060/01.
Sky Sofa in Trezzini Ocean F1060/01.
Red leather Jasper Morrison Low Pad chair.
White Kose ceramics.

Page 163
Long Sky Stool in Ily Scarlet F1067/03.
Red Eros chair by Phillipe Stark.

Page 166-7
Striped curtains and Wave chair in Bokashi
    Persimmon F1083/04.
Printed curtain in Nami Scarlet F1076/01.
Space sofa in Mezzola Persimmon F1090/21.
Wave chair and stool in Nami Slate F1076/02.
Long white Solo Table by B&B Italia.

Pages 172-3
Silk curtains in Francia Poppy F1105/07.
Printed curtain in China Rose Cassis
    F1094/02.
Antique stool covered in Pavlosk Crocus
    F1064/02.
Two seat Square cut velvet sofa in Zilleri Peony
    F1103/03.
Two seat Square cut velvet sofa in Cordellina
    Peony F1100/02.

Pages 178-9
Printed fabric banner in Mirabeau Peony
    F1123/01.
Three seat Square sofa in Mazarin Peony
    F1119/02 with seat cushions in
    Brera Peony F562/45.
Long white Le Banc table by MDF Italia.
Jasper Morrison Low Pad chairs in black leather
    and white leather.

AUTHOR'S ACKNOWLEDGMENTS

Thankyou again to our brilliant team as we work together
again on another book:

Elspeth Thompson
Meryl Lloyd
James Merrell
Anne Furniss
and to my extraordinary 'right hand' Jo Willer

Thank you also to all those at Designers Guild for their
continued support and commitment and to the following
people who have participated in making this book possible:

Nadine Bazaar
Sarah Airey
Liza Grimmond
Ghislaine Jamois
Arne Maynard
Exeter Street Bakery
Liz Wolf Cohen
Georgia Wagner
Ciara O'Flanagan
Richard Polo
Marissa Tuazon
Amanda Back

Tricia Guild's creative manager Jo Willer
Project editor Anne Furniss
Design Meryl Lloyd
Picture research Nadine Bazar, Sarah Airey
Design co-ordinator Ros Holder
Production Beverley Richardson, Vincent Smith
Artwork production and typesetting redbus 020 8560 9774

First published in 2004 by
Quadrille Publishing Limited
Alhambra House
27-31 Charing Cross Road
London WC2H OLS

© Text Elspeth Thompson and Tricia Guild 2004
© Design and layouts Quadrille Publishing Ltd 2004

All rights reserved.

British Library in Cataloguing in Publication Data
A catalogue record for this book is available from the
British Library

ISBN 1844001105

Printed in Hong Kong

a flower full of beauty – Lola